MW00438788

Y O U   # 1964 #   T H I S

MILESTONES, MEMORIES,
TRIVIA AND FACTS, NEWS EVENTS,
PROMINENT PERSONALITIES &
SPORTS HIGHLIGHTS OF THE YEAR

TO :
_____

FROM :
_____

MESSAGE :
_____

_____

selected and researched
by
mary a. pradt

W A R N E R ⬤ T R E A S U R E S ™

PUBLISHED BY WARNER BOOKS

A TIME WARNER COMPANY

Warner Books, Inc.
1271 Avenue of the Americas
New York, New York 10020

Warner Treasures is a
trademark of Warner Books, Inc.

Ⓦ A Time Warner Company

DESIGN:
CAROL BOKUNIEWICZ DESIGN
PRINTED IN SINGAPORE
FIRST PRINTING : MAY 1995
10 9 8 7 6 5 4 3 2 1
ISBN : 0-446-91041-4

Blacks and whites together started agitating for voting rights and other civil rights.

lyndon baines johnson

immediately made his mark with two domestic initiatives: the Civil Rights Act of 1964 and the War on Poverty. He also led the nation deeper into the Vietnam conflict. In August, after a Communist attack on American ships off the coast of North Vietnam, LBJ appealed to Congress for a resolution to allow American forces to defend themselves. The Gulf of Tonkin resolution, which passed through both houses almost unanimously, proved to be the legal foundation for the escalation of the Vietnam conflict. 136 American military personnel died that year. General Westmoreland took command. Americans returned Johnson to the White House in November, when he defeated the Republican challenger Barry Goldwater in a landslide. The election featured the infamous "Daisy" commercial by the Johnson campaign, which vaguely associated Goldwater with the use of nuclear weapons.

Stirrings of the student protest movement began in Berkeley, California, where students took a page from civil rights activists and staged sit–ins in university buildings there. Demonstrations also dampened festivities at the World's Fair in New York City, and it was Freedom Summer in Mississippi and elsewhere in the South.

robert kennedy's earlier effort to purge labor of organized crime culminated in the sentencing of Jimmy Hoffa, the president of the Teamsters Union, to eight years in prison. Bobby Kennedy resigned later in the year to run for a U.S. Senate seat in New York.

newsreel

One of the largest jewel heists in history took place in October 1964, as the Star of India sapphire was spirited away from its home at the Museum of Natural History in New York City. It wasn't to be recovered until the following year. Life imitates art: *the pink panther* premiered.

headlines

In the Kremlin, Nikita Khrushchev lost his grip on power and was ousted as leader of the Communist party in the Soviet Union. Leonid Brezhnev was tapped to succeed Khrushchev. It was expected that Brezhnev would begin to repair the strained relationship between Russia and Communist China, which became the newest member of the Nuclear Bomb club. Brezhnev continued the cozy relationship with Fidel Castro's Cuba.

SEIZE REVERE
CITY RECORDS

KIDNAP MANAGER
OF MOVIE HOUSE

LINK GROVE
IN TRADE BY
THE RED SOX

The Boston

COL.
RETUR

HOUSE FRONT OF
YELLOW IRKS HU

5

The nightclub

whiskey–a–go–go

opened in Los Angeles.
Folks allegedly danced
the **WATUSI** there.

GENERAL FOODS
DEBUTED THE FIRST
**FREEZE–DRIED
COFFEE.**

**The first movies were
shown on airline flights.**

Nightclub comedian **LENNY BRUCE,** 37, faced yet another obscenity charge in 1964. His heroin addiction cost him his life, but he was the most important influence on comedy as a medium of expression in the second half of the century.

cultural
milestones

dr. martin luther king, jr.,

was awarded the Nobel Peace Prize, and Jean-Paul Sartre won the Nobel Prize for Literature.

THE 400TH BIRTHDAY OF WILLIAM SHAKESPEARE WAS CELEBRATED.

troll dolls appeared on students' desks throughout the nation. They were soon stamped out, only to reappear in other decades.

There were 51,600,000 TV households in America, over 92 percent. Only 1.6 million households, however, had color sets — just 3.1% of TV households.

television

top-rated shows of the fall 1964 season:

1. "Bonanza" (NBC)

2. "Bewitched" (ABC)

3. "Gomer Pyle, U.S.M.C." (CBS)

4. "The Andy Griffith Show" (CBS)

5. "The Fugitive" (ABC)

6. "The Red Skelton Hour" (CBS)

7. "The Dick Van Dyke Show" (CBS)

8. "The Lucy Show" (CBS)

9. "Peyton Place II" (ABC)

10. "Combat" (ABC)

THIS WAS PERNELL ROBERTS'S LAST YEAR IN THE SADDLE AS ADAM CARTWRIGHT ON "BONANZA."

ALSO POPULAR WERE "WALT DISNEY'S WONDERFUL WORLD OF COLOR," "THE BEVERLY HILLBILLIES," "MY THREE SONS," "LASSIE," "THE MUNSTERS," AND "GILLIGAN'S ISLAND."

FOR THE KIDS
"The Famous Adventures of Mr. Magoo" aired Saturdays at 8:00 A.M. on NBC.

milestones

celeb wedding of the year

On March 5, **ELIZABETH TAYLOR,** 32, was granted a divorce in Puerto Vallarta, Mexico, from crooner Eddie Fisher, 35, on grounds of abandonment. Miss Taylor was awarded custody of their adopted daughter, Lisa Todd. On March 15, she married actor **RICHARD BURTON,** 38, in Montreal. It was her fifth marriage, Burton's second.

'64

births

ROB LOWE, actor who proved overexposed by a home-made video, was born on March 17, 1964.

MELISSA GILBERT, star of "Little House on the Prairie," was born on May 8.

ROBIN GIVENS, actress and ex-wife of boxer and convicted rapist Mike Tyson, was born on November 27.

PRINCE EDWARD OF ENGLAND was born on March 10.

MATT DILLON, actor, came into the world on February 18.

JOSE CANSECO, baseball and onetime Madonna paramour, was born on July 2.

BONNIE BLAIR, speed skater and Olympic medalist, was born on March 18.

D E A T H S

Rachel Carson,
Silent Spring author, died at 56.

Spike Jones,
irreverent composer and band leader, died.

Gracie Allen,
vaudeville star of the "George Burns and Gracie Allen Show," died in August at 58.

Alan Ladd,
actor, star of "This Gun for Hire" and "Shane" died.

Peter Lorre,
actor, best known for his fiendish roles in "M" and "The Maltese Falcon," died.

General Douglas MacArthur,
war hero relieved of his command by Truman, died in April at age 84.

Herbert Clark Hoover,
president (1928–32), died at 90.

Jawaharlal Nehru,
India's first Prime Minister, died of a heart attack at 74 in May.

Cole Porter,
composer and lyricist of "You're the Top," "I Get a Kick Out of You," etc., died.

Cole Porter

'64

1. **i want to hold your hand**
   beatles
2. **can't buy me love**
   beatles
3. **there i've said it again**
   bobby vinton
4. **baby love**
   supremes
5. **pretty woman**
   roy orbison

6. **the house of the rising sun**
   animals
7. **chapel of love**
   dixie cups
8. **i feel fine**
   beatles
9. **she loves you**
   beatles
10. **my guy**
    mary wells

hit music

other top singles included:

"I Get Around" (Beach Boys)
"Come See About Me" (Supremes)
"Where Did Our Love Go?" (Supremes)
"Do Wah Diddy Diddy" (Manfred Mann)
"Everybody Loves Somebody" (Dean Martin)
"Leader of the Pack" (Shangri–Las)
"People" (Barbra Streisand)
"The Girl from Ipanema" (Stan Getz and Astrud Gilberto)
"Under the Boardwalk" (Drifters)

OTHER HOT ACTS INCLUDED GENE PITNEY, RICK NELSON, LITTLE ANTHONY AND THE IMPERIALS, THE DAVE CLARK FIVE, DIONNE WARWICK, MARTHA AND THE VANDELLAS, BOBBY GOLDSBORO, ELVIS, THE TEMPTATIONS, HERMAN'S HERMITS, THE FOUR SEASONS, AND GERRY AND THE PACEMAKERS.

In February, four young men spearheaded what was to be known as the British Invasion. "I Want to Hold Your Hand" proved to be the first of many hits the Beatles were to have in America that year.

other beatles singles on the 1964 charts included:

"A Hard Day's Night"
"Love Me Do"
"Twist and Shout"
"Do You Want to Know a Secret"
"Please Please Me"
"P.S. I Love You"
"And I Love Her"
"I Saw Her Standing There"
and "She's a Woman"

fiction

1. **the spy who came in from the cold**
   john le carré

2. **candy**
   terry southern

3. **herzog**
   saul bellow

4. **armegeddon**
   leon uris

5. **the man**
   irving wallace

6. **the rector of justin**
   louis auchincloss

7. **the martyred**
   richard e. kim

8. **you only live twice**
   ian fleming

9. **this rough magic**
   mary stewart

10. **convention**
    fletcher knebel

bestselling

SAUL BELLOW'S *HERZOG* HAS THE DISTINCTION OF HAVING THE LONGEST RUN ON THE BESTSELLER LIST BY A NOBEL PRIZE WINNER.

nonfiction

books

CASSIUS CLAY defeated Sonny Liston to become the world heavyweight champion of boxing. "They all must fall/in the round I call," Clay quipped. Later in the year he would be known as

muhammad ali

BILL BRADLEY, Princeton basketball star, turned down a chance to turn pro in December 1964. He would have been a first-choice draft pick for the New York Knicks and would have commanded a salary of at least $200,000 a year. Bradley chose to attend Oxford as a Rhodes scholar. He said that athletes retire at 30 "with nothing more than a scrapbook of their clippings." He went on to become both a New York Knicks star *and* a U.S. senator.

Jim Brown and the Cleveland Browns won the National Football League championship, beating the Colts 27-0. In the fledgling American Football League, yes, once upon a time the Buffalo Bills did win the big one, but before there was a Super Bowl. They beat the Boston Patriots for the AFL championship.

sports

A. J. FOYT WON THE INDIANAPOLIS 500, AMIDST TRAGEDY AT THE BRICKYARD, WHEN EDDIE SACHS AND DAVE MACDONALD WERE KILLED IN AN ACCIDENT EARLY IN THE RACE.

EVEN WITHOUT BOB COUSY, THE CELTICS KEPT WINNING CHAMPIONSHIPS, INCLUDING THEIR 6TH STRAIGHT NBA TITLE.

BASEBALL

The St. Louis Cardinals beat the New York Yankees in a 7-game series in 1964. The regular season featured the Father's Day perfect game, pitched by Philadelphia's Jim Bunning against the New York Mets.

17

peter sellers

had four roles of note in 1964, three of which were in *Dr. Strangelove.*

My Fair Lady was the big winner in 1964. It won Oscars for Best Picture, Best Actor, cinematography, art direction, and costume design. Other nominees for Best Picture were: *Becket, Dr. Strangelove, or How I Learned to Stop Worrying and Love the Bomb, Mary Poppins,* and *Zorba the Greek.* **Julie Andrews** won the Oscar as Best Actress in *Mary Poppins,* over Anne Bancroft (*The Pumpkin Eater*), Sophia Loren (*Marriage Italian Style*), Debbie Reynolds (*The Unsinkable Molly Brown*), and Kim Stanley (*Seance on a Wet Afternoon*). **Rex Harrison** won out over Richard Burton and Peter O'Toole in *Becket,* Anthony Quinn as *Zorba the Greek,* and Peter Sellers in *Dr. Strangelove.* **Peter Ustinov** won Best Supporting Actor honors, for *Topkapi,* a jewel heist film. **Lila Kedrova** won Best Supporting Actress for her *Zorba* role. **Mary Poppins** snared several Oscars, including Best Song for "Chim Chim Cheree." The Italian production **Yesterday, Today, and Tomorrow** was named Best Foreign Language Film.

top box-office grosses of the year

1. *The Carpetbaggers* ($13,000,000)
2. *It's a Mad, Mad, Mad, Mad World* ($10,000,000)
3. *The Unsinkable Molly Brown* ($7,500,000)
4. *Charade* ($6,150,000)
5. *The Cardinal* ($5,275,000)

THE AVERAGE COST OF A MOVIE TICKET IN 1964 WAS 92.5 CENTS.

movies

top box-office stars of 1964

Doris Day	Elvis Presley
Jack Lemmon	Shirley MacLaine
Rock Hudson	Ann–Margret
John Wayne	Paul Newman
Cary Grant	Richard Burton

19

It was the third record-breaking year in a row for American carmakers. Sales were close to the 8-million mark. There were 334 different models offered. Especially

cars

notable new entries were the Plymouth Barracuda fastback and the Ford Mustang sports car. The Barracuda boasted a sloping rear deck and fold-down rear seat, to provide a lot of carrying space or even a sleeping space.

'64

THE FORD MUSTANG, WITH EUROPEAN SPORTSCAR STYLING, PROVED ONE OF THE ALL-TIME MOST POPULAR AMERICAN CARS.

Ford Mustang Hardtop

New
Ford Mustang
$2368* f.o.b. Detroit

This is the car you never expected from Detroit. Mustang is so distinctively beautiful it has received the Tiffany Award for Excellence in American Design...the first time an automobile has been honored with the Tiffany Gold Medal. You can own the Mustang hardtop for a suggested retail price of just $2,368—f.o.b. Detroit. This does not include destination charges from Detroit, options, state and local taxes and fees, if any. Whitewall tires are $33.90 extra.

Every Mustang includes these luxury features unavailable—or available only at extra cost—in most other cars: bucket seats; wall-to-wall carpeting; all-vinyl upholstery; padded instrument panel; and full wheel covers. Also standard: floor-shift; courtesy lights; sports steering wheel; front arm rests; a 170 cu. in. Six, and much more.

That's the Mustang hardtop. With its four-passenger roominess and surprisingly spacious trunk, it will be an ideal car for many families. Yet Mustang is designed to be designed by you. For instance, the trip to the supermarket can be a lot more fun when you add convenience options like power brakes or steering, Cruise-O-Matic transmission, push-button radio, 260 cu. in. V-8.

Or, you can design Mustang to suit your special taste for elegance with such luxury refinements as: air conditioning; vinyl-covered roof; full-length console; accent paint-stripe, and convertible with power top.

If you're looking for action, Mustang's the place to find it, with a 289 cu. in. V-8; 4-speed fully synchronized transmission; Rally-Pac (tachometer and clock) and other exciting options.

For an authentic scale model of the new Ford Mustang, send $1.00 to Mustang Offer, Department A-1, P.O. Box 35, Troy, Michigan. (Offer ends July 31, 1964)

TRY TOTAL PERFORMANCE FOR A CHANGE!

FORD

Mustang · Falcon · Fairlane · Ford · Thunderbird

21

Above-the-knee hemlines were accepted almost everywhere. Colored tights and textured stockings helped. Tight toreador pants gave way to longer, pipestem styling. Chanel and Norell did dressier pants looks. There were a few "ethnic" influences, like burnooses, caftans, tunics, and sari-inspired flowing garments. For evening, *the* look was the discotheque dress, short, bare, swingy at the hemline.

fashion

the topless bathing suit

premiered, courtesy of
Rudi Gernreich, as did
the transparent blouse.

More talked about than worn

**THE BODY STOCKING
was introduced and
was an instant success.**

23

final factoid

In November, ABC pitted **LES CRANE** against **JOHNNY CARSON** in the late-night talk-show schedule. Carson won.

archive photos: inside front cover, pages 1, 5, 7, 10, 15, 22, 23, inside back cover.

associated press: pages 2, 6, 16, 17, 23.

photofest: pages 3, 8, 9, 11, 13, 18, 19, 25.

photo research:
alice albert

coordination:
rustyn birch

design:
carol bokuniewicz design
mutsumi hyuga

'64